Brook Study Guide

COMPARATIVE STUDY NOTES

CRACK THE COMPARATIVE #5

Victoria Kennefick

Amy Farrell

SCENE BY SCENE
WICKLOW, IRELAND

Scene by Scene
Wicklow, Ireland.
www.scenebyscene.ie

Brooklyn Study Guide by Amy Farrell.
ISBN 978-1-910949-82-5

Cover Image © Mayya Abdullayeva

Contents

About This Book

This book is a study guide for Leaving Certificate English students studying *Brooklyn* as part of the Comparative Study.

There are notes and analysis of key moments for Cultural Context/ Social Setting, Literary Genre, General Vision and Viewpoint, Theme/Issue (Relationships) and Hero, Heroine, Villain.

I have selected key moments to analyse for each comparative study mode. However, my choices are not definitive - any moment can be considered and explored for any mode. Feel free to consider other moments to add to your analysis for the comparative study.

Brooklyn by John Crowley

Brooklyn follows the story of Eilis Lacey as she emigrates to New York and falls in love. The tragic loss of her sister forces her to return home, where she must choose which man, and which life, she wants.

Cultural Context/Social Setting

Cultural Context/Social Setting refers to the world of the text. Think about social norms, beliefs, values and attitudes.

Brooklyn is set in the 1950s, in both Enniscorthy and New York. This historical era impacts heavily on characters' circumstances and attitudes.

This is a story of **emigration**, and the difficulties of leaving behind everything that is familiar and starting a new life in a new place. **Eilis' move to America** is so significant because of the length of **the journey**, which **makes home very far away**. Her reason for making such a move tells us a lot about her world, **if she stays at home she will not have the opportunities or employment choices she does in New York**.

At first **she finds New York to be desperately lonely**, despite lodging in a house full of young Irish women. She feels the distance from home keenly, as seen in her eager wait for letters from home.

The influence and **importance of the Catholic Church** is a part of the cultural backdrop of this text. It is Father Flood, a Catholic priest, who has arranged Eilis' emigration, demonstrating his **central role in the community**. Eilis' involvement in his charity Christmas dinner shows the significant role the Church plays in caring for the forgotten Irish of New York. The importance of the Church in characters' lives is underscored by Nancy and George's church wedding, a public event, involving a large number of members of the local community.

Marriage is central to society in this world. Women eagerly search for husbands, as we see with Eilis' friend Nancy, her cabin mate Georgina onboard the passenger liner to America, and with Eilis herself, as she goes to dances hoping to find a boyfriend. **Finding a suitable man is what women aspire to**, as the lodging house dinner time conversation illustrates. Once Eilis is involved with Tony, her housemates have more to talk to her about, and more to share with her - she has become one of them, a young woman hoping to marry.

There is a **sense of permanence to marriage** in this world. Tony marries Eilis, in part, to secure her return to New York. He knows that a **commitment** like this will ensure that she does not stay in Ireland when she goes home to her grieving mother.

Eilis' mother also prioritises marriage, happily anticipating a match between Eilis and Jim, **eager to have her daughter married and settled** in Enniscorthy. **Marriage is fundamental** in these characters' lives, it is viewed as **a necessary part of a fulfilling life**.

The significance and importance of marriage in their world may help to explain why Eilis' mother cannot speak to her when Eilis opens up about having a husband in New York. This is a **huge secret** to have kept from her own mother, and **her relationship with Jim is a betrayal** of her vows to her husband.

Her secret marriage explains Eilis' hasty return to Brooklyn. Miss Kelly now knows she is married, and **rumours and gossip** are sure to circulate in this small town. **By leaving, Eilis escapes this small town's judgement**, and gets to return to **a world of potential and possibility in New York**.

Eilis also manages to escape admitting to her husband that she was involved with another man, as **due to the great distance between them, Tony knows nothing of Jim** and his affection for Eilis. She can use being so separate from her homeplace and family to her advantage, as it allows her to conceal her relationship with Jim and look forward to a bright future with Tony and his plans of children, building a home, and setting up his own business. **Eilis' world is a place where she can make a fresh start** in her life, unhindered by her past.

Cultural Context/Social Setting
Key Moments

Working in Miss Kelly's Shop

Eilis attends early morning mass before working in Miss Kelly's shop on Sunday morning. The shop is crowded after mass, full of locals jostling as they wait to be served.

Miss Kelly orders Eilis to serve Mrs Brady (a wealthy woman) next, even though she is not next in the queue. Miss Kelly is more interested in looking after her well-to-do customers, **social standing is seen to be very significant here**.

Eilis does as she is told, **Miss Kelly's position** of shop owner **gives her power and authority. This is the social norm, that Miss Kelly look**

after those she views as important.

When a customer asks to purchase shoe polish, Miss Kelly mocks her, saying it is not a Sunday item and that she could have done with it before now. Her **judgemental attitude** gives an insight into life in this small town where **everyone knows everyone else's business**.

Advice from Georgina on the Passenger Liner

Georgina, Eilis' cabin mate, offers her advice about life onboard, and at immigration control once they land in America. Having made the crossing before, Georgina is more experienced and wiser than Eilis. Georgina's help here shows that there is warmth and support in this society, even from strangers.

Georgina tells Eilis how to take control of the shared toilet onboard, showing Eilis the right way to do things. The underlying message here is that **one must be smart and savvy** and not let themselves get pushed around or taken for a fool if they are to thrive.

Georgina also tells Eilis what to do in **immigration control** when they disembark. The focus here is on being composed, confident, and **acting like an American**. It seems if Eilis is to be successful in this new world she will have to embrace it wholeheartedly, and work determinedly to understand how this society works. Georgina is matter of fact about the rules of this new place, **success here is clearly defined as 'American'**.

Father Flood's Christmas Dinner

Father Flood's annual Christmas dinner for the forgotten Irish men

of New York gives a poignant insight into the sometimes unhappy
reality of emigration. These aged men are lonely and forgotten now that
their youth and strength is spent. New York is a lonely, unforgiving
place for them. These men are trapped in their failed lives, with
nothing at home to return to, and nothing for them in this land far from
home.

Father Flood interrupts the revelry, asking the men to thank the ladies
for their hard day's work. By way of thanks, Frankie sings a haunting song as
gaeilge, reminding us of these men's Irish roots and all that they have lost
through emigration and their failure to make successful lives for themselves
in America. They are dressed in old shirts, jackets and flat caps, just as they
would be at home in Ireland. Their separation from, and belonging to
Ireland are both apparent as they drink and celebrate Christmas.

Rose's Death

Rose's death makes clear just how far from home Eilis is. The news
of her sister's death is broken to her by Father Flood. His high standing and
respected position in the community makes this sad task his responsibility.

Eilis will miss her sister's funeral, as she is too far away to make the
lengthy journey in time, a fact underscored by her scheduled transatlantic
phone call with her mother.

Rose's death makes clear the physical distance between
Enniscorthy and New York, but also how separate Eilis' new life
is. She has missed the last weeks of her sister's life, a huge price to pay for
emigrating.

Rose's death also makes clear the sense of responsibility and

duty towards her mother that Eilis feels. Eilis' mother is now alone, without family to comfort or support her. Eilis decides that she must return to Ireland because her mother would feel better if she were with her. The **importance of family** is clear as Eilis decides to return home to be with her mother, despite her flourishing relationship with Tony and her happiness with her new life. **Duty** is what motivates her here, giving an insight into how highly family is valued and respected in this world.

Nancy and George's Wedding

Nancy and George get married in the local church in front of all their friends and family. This is a **public, church affair that shows the importance of marriage to these characters**. As a young couple in love, **getting married is the logical path for their relationship to follow**, showing that this is a **traditional world where marriage is valued.**

This event shows the importance of the church, as Nancy and George choose to get married here. Perhaps this tells us that **Ireland is more traditional than New York, where Eilis wed Tony at City Hall.**

After the ceremony an older woman chats to Eilis, suggesting that soon Eilis will marry Jim. It appears that this is **a place of rumour, gossip and speculation, where neighbours keep an eye on one another's business**. Also, this woman feels she can make these assumptions about Eilis and Jim and speak to her of them. It would appear that **talking to others about their private or personal affairs is routine in Enniscorthy.**

Miss Kelly Confronts Eilis

Eilis' confrontation with Miss Kelly in the older woman's shop reveals how small-minded, nosy and spiteful people can be in this world.

Miss Kelly has sent for Eilis to dominate and speak down to her, feeling superior because she has discovered that Eilis has secretly wed. She begins by telling Eilis that she has heard she is working in Davis's and that **there is lots of talk about her and young Jim Farrell.** It is clear that in this world, people talk and **gossip** about one another.

This becomes more apparent when Miss Kelly reveals that **she has learned of Eilis' marriage via Mrs Brady's niece who is also living in Brooklyn.** She remarks to Eilis that **the world is a small place,** delighting in her discovery.

Eilis replies that she had forgotten what this town is like, **highlighting the petty, small-minded outlook** of Miss Kelly and those like her.

Eilis asks Miss Kelly what she thought she was going to do with this knowledge, and the older woman does not seem to know. Miss Kelly had not thought past the childish one-upmanship of knowing personal details of Eilis' life. **Gossip and rumour are the norm here, with characters like Miss Kelly hungry to discover what they can.**

Literary Genre

Literary Genre focuses on the ways that texts tell their stories. When analysing Literary Genre, consider the choices the author makes in telling their story this way, and how this impacts on the reader's experience of the story. Think about aspects of narration such as the manner and style of narration, characterisation, setting, use of conflict, tension, other literary techniques, etc.

The **film format** appeals to the senses as it has **both visual and audio dimensions**, and is a **very immersive way of experiencing a story**. The story benefits from the audience being able to see and hear characters, and respond emotionally to what is portrayed onscreen. The soundtrack is influential in creating mood and feeling, and so has an emotional impact on the audience.

Eilis' character grows and develops over the course of the film. She is **transformed** from a naive, inexperienced girl, into an assertive, independent woman. She changes from behaving in a way that pleases others, such as quietly accepting Miss Kelly's poor treatment in her shop, to choosing her own path in life, and deciding to return to Tony and New York, despite the fact that this choice disappoints her mother. **Eilis' character, and how she grows and matures, is a compelling aspect of the narrative.**

From a character perspective, it is **significant that both Tony and Jim are good men, with much to offer Eilis**. Tony is warm and passionate, and wants to set up his own business, build a house and have children with Eilis. He offers her a world of potential and possibility, a new life. Jim, though more reserved, is also a kind, warm-hearted character, who wants to share his life with Eilis. His large home and wealth add to what he can offer

Eilis. **The fact that both of these characters are kind and loving with a lot to offer complicates Eilis' choice and adds tension to the plotline.** It is very engaging and involving, as a viewer, to wonder which man, and so which life, Eilis will choose. **This choice adds excitement and drama to the story.**

Conflict also makes this text exciting. **Eilis' inner conflict** over which man and life to choose makes the story more tense and exciting.

Conflict in the form of confrontation also adds to the story's excitement and appeal. When Miss Kelly attempts to expose Eilis as a married woman, it is exciting and satisfying to see Eilis stand up to her former boss and defiantly call herself Eilis Fiorello. In this way, **conflict heightens the excitement** of the text, and **adds to our admiration of Eilis' character.**

The **structure of the film encourages the audience to respond positively to Eilis. Most of the film is composed of one on one conversations**, where Eilis exchanges dialogue with one other character. These exchanges create the feeling that **we are there with Eilis**, part of her life, involved in her journey, meeting these people as she does. **Her perspective is our perspective**, we only see what she sees, and scenes where she is alone with her thoughts and feelings add to the sense that this is her story that we are witnessing. **Eilis is in virtually every scene, adding to the connection the viewer has with her**.

The viewer's connection to the story is Eilis, and this has a big impact on **the story's ending.** We do not dwell on the unhappiness of Eilis' mother as Eilis leaves once more, nor do we spend too long feeling sorry for Jim who has been rejected in favour of Tony. Rather, **the viewer is with Eilis, heading back to New York, focused on her future, just as she is.** The **happy ending** would be impossible if the viewer did not share Eilis' perspective, and were to dwell on how things have gone wrong at home. **Crucially, this is a happy ending because we see it through Eilis' eyes**, with the confusion and sadness of Enniscorthy left far behind.

It is worth considering the **symbolism** and **visual imagery** that adds to the storytelling in *Brooklyn*. **Eilis' voyage to New York is both a literal and symbolic journey**, as once in Brooklyn, she will begin her new life. As she steps out of immigration the doorway is illuminated with light, stressing the potential and hopefulness of her life in this new world.

Colour impacts on the imagery in the text. When Eilis visits Father Flood in the spring she wears a bright, yellow dress and Father Flood remarks that she is very changed from the miserable girl who first arrived in New York. The colour of Eilis' costume communicates her feelings and outlook to the audience.

When Eilis receives the news of her sister's death the colours are dark and muted. She wears black, as does Father Flood, and they sit in a quiet, dark room. The colours here communicate how the characters feel, full of sadness and grief.

Indeed, to a certain degree, **Eilis' character growth can be charted through the outfits she wears**. Before she leaves Enniscorthy, Rose wishes that Eilis had some better clothes, when she returns to her hometown her clothing reminds the viewer that she is not the same girl who left Enniscorthy all those weeks ago. Her outfits are more fashionable than those of the women of Enniscorthy, she wears stylish sunglasses, and has learned the trick of wearing her swimming costume under her clothes when she visits the beach with her friends. In this way, **the audience are subtly reminded of Eilis' growth** over the course of the film by her changing wardrobe.

In the film's final scene, Eilis and Tony are joyfully reunited in the Brooklyn sunshine. Once again, **light and bright colour** helps to tell the story, adding to the **happy ending**.

Literary Genre
Key Moments

Eilis' Departure

Eilis' departure adds a lot to the story. As she stands on deck, surrounded by strangers, the wide expanse of **clear, blue sky behind her suggests hope and possibility. Contrasted with this are the sad, concerned faces below her** of those left behind, including her mother and sister.

In this scene, **Eilis does not speak**, her **trepidation and uncertainty are communicated through her facial expressions**. She stands onboard and blows a kiss to her sister, who must hurry after their mother, leaving Eilis. Neither Eilis or Rose cry openly as they struggle to hold themselves together, but their sadness is very apparent. This is a **poignant moment** that **makes the audience aware of all that Eilis is leaving behind**, and the **uncertainty of what lies before her**. It is an **emotionally rich moment**, communicating anxiety and sadness, while also moving the **plot** into the next phase of the story.

Rose's Death

Rose's death is one of the most significant events in the film from a

plot perspective. It is due to the loss of Rose that Eilis feels duty bound to return to Ireland and her mother, and while at home she will find herself falling into a relationship with Jim Farrell, a major **complication** bringing **suspense** to the story.

Rose's death immediately follows Eilis and Tony's visit to Coney Island. The viewer is realising how good life can be for Eilis in New York. As Eilis narrates a letter home, we see her mother discover Rose's body, and so learn of Rose's death moments before Eilis does. Her mother's grief and the sorrowful music changes the mood completely, to one of loss and sadness.

As Father Flood and Eilis' manager approach her, her breath quickens; she knows they bear bad news. It is Father Flood, dressed in black, that delivers the sad news to Eilis. All is quiet in the room, as Eilis comes to terms with missing Rose's funeral and the fact that she will never see her sister again. **This is a low point for Eilis, as she questions why she ever came to New York. This scene is marked by dark colours, quiet and stillness, creating a sense of loss and mourning.**

Tony's Proposal

Eilis and Tony's hasty plan to secretly marry is an **exciting moment** in the film, while also being an extremely **significant plot point**.

When Eilis tells Tony she must go home to Ireland he asks her to marry him before she leaves. She asks if he does not trust her to come back, **foreshadowing her relationship with Jim** once she is home. Tony wants to marry her quickly, and secretly, saying that if they don't he will go crazy. **This scene reveals a lot about Tony's character, and their relationship.** He is interested in what he wants, putting pressure on Eilis to agree to marry. What may be passion and spontaneity on Tony's part could also be interpreted as controlling manipulation, and a way to force Eilis' return. She is slow to decide, uncertain about marrying, but agrees to before they go and spend the night together, thus **further cementing their relationship**.

In this moment we see how **Eilis is eager to please Tony**, allowing him to influence her and make this huge decision.

This secret marriage will be very significant when Eilis returns home and has the chance to start a new life in Enniscorthy with Jim Farrell. It will provide much **inner conflict** for Eilis, as she wrestles with her difficult choice, and her **secrecy will demonstrate the rift between Eilis and her life at home**.

Nancy and George's Wedding

Nancy and George's wedding marks a significant moment in the narrative for a number of reasons. Their **public celebration** stresses the importance and **significance of marriage** in these characters' lives. It is not something to be taken lightly, and so the **tension is increased** surrounding Eilis' choice. As Eilis sits in the church, listening to Nancy and George exchanging their vows, she looks **solemn, inwardly troubled** by the weight of her own secret vows. Jim sits beside her and glances at Eilis. It appears that his mind is also on marriage, thus further increasing the **tension** and making Eilis' decision more pressing and urgent.

After the ceremony an older woman suggests that it will not be long until Eilis and Jim wed, another **subtle increase in tension**. This scene **gradually increases the pressure that Eilis is under**, it feels like marriage to Jim is imminent.

As Eilis dances in Jim's arms at the wedding dance, he tells her that they need to talk, and promises that he will soon propose. She does not give him a direct answer, but leans into him, clearly **torn and confused** about what she should do. This further **increases the tension** for the viewer, as it is obvious that this situation cannot go on much longer. **Eilis needs to make a decision and break somebody's heart.**

Confrontation with Miss Kelly

Eilis being sent for by Miss Kelly signals that something is about to happen, the audience eagerly anticipates a **plot development**.

Miss Kelly is in control of the situation, inviting Eilis to sit and asking her questions based on what she has heard of her. Eilis sits silently for much of this exchange, letting Miss Kelly speak. When Miss Kelly tells her about an Enniscorthy girl getting married in City Hall, Eilis is evasive, but Miss Kelly presses on, suggesting that Eilis' name is now something Italian. **There is a close up of Eilis' face as she decides what to do, whether to own her past or deny Tony. This is a tense moment, as the truth of Eilis' secret marriage is about to be revealed.**

Eilis rises to Miss Kelly's challenge here, asking her what she was planning to do with what she knows. Eilis is calm and reasonable, and she completely deflates Miss Kelly. She stands to leave and calls herself Eilis Fiorello, **claiming her married name publicly for the first time. This marks a change in Eilis' character, she is assertive and confident, and has finally chosen her path.** This feels like a **triumphant moment** as Eilis bests her former boss and asserts herself.

Eilis Tells her Mother she is Returning to New York

Eilis is tearful at dinner, what she is about to tell her mother, and leaving her again, weighs heavily on her. The audience see that **Eilis is a caring, emotional character, who never intended to cause hurt by her actions**.

Eilis' mother does not appear to cope with her daughter's news of marriage and return to New York. Perhaps it is her personal grief and loss that stops her from being able to talk to Eilis about her husband.

However, from a viewer's perspective, Eilis' mother's actions may be interpreted as cold and unfeeling. As she bids her daughter goodbye, we may feel that **Eilis is right to leave this place** and her difficult relationship with her mother behind.

The **pace** is increasing now that the truth about Eilis' marriage has been revealed, **moving the story towards its conclusion**.

General Vision and Viewpoint

**Focus on the overall outlook of the text and whether it is dark and hopeless or optimistic and uplifting.
How does this text make you feel about life?**

Brooklyn **is a positive, hopeful and uplifting text, as it is a love story and story of self discovery. However, life is not without its difficulties and problems for Eilis.**

Initially, Eilis struggles after emigrating to New York, finding this huge change in her life very difficult. She is conflicted about the move to Brooklyn. She knows it is for the best, but does not seem to enjoy herself. Indeed, she suffers terribly from homesickness and surrounds herself with the world of home in the form of Ma Kehoe's boarding house and Father Flood's charitable Christmas dinner. **Her emigration is a struggle**, she is **isolated and alone**, longing to be with her family. However, **she perseveres and is rewarded, showing a positive outlook and perspective**. She overcomes her homesickness and loneliness and secures a good job, a fulfilling education (which further improves her prospects) and falls in love with a young man with high hopes and dreams for their future together. **In New York, Eilis' future looks bright and full of potential**.

Indeed, **when she returns to Enniscorthy, Eilis' future also looks bright** as she works at Davis's, enjoys spending time with her mother and friend Nancy, and falls in love with the eligible and available Jim Farrell. Here too, **Eilis has the potential and promise of future happiness. The worldview is bright and positive on both counts, as each choice suggests that Eilis may be very happy.**

What is perhaps more troubling is Eilis' duplicitous nature and indecisiveness. The idea that she is betraying and misleading these men that she supposedly loves adds a **sense of negativity** to the worldview. It is **difficult to view her romances as completely positive when one is aware that she is unfaithful**, misleading these men that love her. **The idea that loving relationships should prove false taints the positive view of life offered in this text.** Eilis' indecision and infidelity suggests that **not even love can be perfect**, one's heart is never safe, a disappointing idea.

However, Eilis' difficulty in choosing a man perhaps suggests that she could be happy with either, showing that **life is full of the potential for**

love and fulfilment. Eilis' choice is difficult as each man is so loving. However, although her predicament is difficult, her life probably will not be. Her future is hopeful, promising a lasting and fulfilling relationship, whichever man she chooses.

Eilis' life becomes her own when she returns to America. At home, she goes along with the decisions and desires of others, trying to please them, as when she allows her mother to imagine a time when Eilis and Jim will be together. In order to be free, to live a truly independent life, Eilis must leave her home behind and find her own place in the world. **The writer presents a worldview where the difficult choice must be made, and hardships endured, in order to achieve personal freedom and autonomy**. For Eilis, New York represents a fresh start. **It is a place of potential, where anything can happen if one is prepared to work hard**.

Interestingly, **love does not conquer all in *Brooklyn*. The worldview on offer is not so simple**. Love is available to Eilis - her family and friends love her, and she is involved with two men who are both devoted to her. However, **it as not as easy as falling in love to ensure happiness**. Rather, **Eilis must choose who and what she wants in life in order to be happy**, she has to switch from being a passenger to being an active participant in her life to be happy and fulfilled.

Overall, Eilis has a wealth of potential and possibility in her life which creates a **positive outlook** and the suggestion that **life's possibilities are endless**.

General Vision and Viewpoint
Key Moments

Leaving Ireland (on deck)

As Eilis stands on deck, looking down on her mother and sister, the **outlook is very mixed**. On one hand, she is about to embark on **an exciting journey to a new country, full of potential and possibility**, a very positive prospect. However, **this journey is tinged with sadness** as Eilis must leave behind her friends, family, and everything she has ever known in order to pursue this new life. The faces in the crowd are serious and unsmiling. This is **not a joyful departure, but a moment of loss for many**.

We see Eilis' mother turn and walk away, reluctantly followed by Rose as Eilis looks on. This moment captures Eilis' loss of home and family at this exciting point of departure. **Although forward looking and hopeful, this scene has an underlying sadness due to Eilis' separation from her family.**

Alone in New York

Eilis is daunted and **overwhelmed by her new life** in New York. We see her struggle to make conversation with a co-worker and a customer. She feels **lost and out of her depth**, showing how trying her new circumstances are for her.

Eilis' manager tells her to treat every customer like a new friend. When Eilis says she will try, she is told that trying is not good enough, it is what she will have to do. Eilis' new job and new life are demanding. We see that **although New York offers her the potential of a new life, it is not necessarily an easy one. Eilis will have to work to make this job, and this life, her own.**

In the next scene we see Eilis eating alone. In this sequence we see that Eilis' new life is not easy at first. She suffers from homesickness, loneliness and isolation, and finds herself in a tough, demanding situation. **This time of adjustment is seen to be difficult, but ultimately, it will be rewarding. Perhaps the director suggests that happiness must be worked for, that life is not easy, but that determination and resilience will pay off.**

Visiting Coney Island with Tony

The episode where Eilis goes to Coney Island with Tony is full of romance and happiness. Eilis and Tony are a young couple in love, free to enjoy all life has to offer.

There is humour in Eilis having to change into her swimming costume under a towel while Tony shyly looks away. Tony's reaction to seeing Eilis in her swimsuit, whistling when he sees her, adds to our sense of their developing romance. Their relationship is further developed when we see them kissing passionately in the sea. **This developing relationship shows that Eilis could be very happy in New York. She has made the adjustment to this new place and is beginning to truly enjoy her life here, making this a positive, optimistic moment.**

Eilis reads a letter to Rose in a voiceover as we see her and Tony kiss. **She writes Rose that for the first time since arriving in America she is really happy. It is clear that her relationship with Tony is what has** brought this happiness into her life, making this a bright moment in the text.

Rose's Death

Rose's death is an extremely low point for Eilis. She sits with Father Flood in a dark room and learns the details of her sister's death, a tragedy that has occurred so far away that **Eilis is cut-off and isolated, even in her grief**.

The secrecy surrounding Rose's illness adds to the bleakness of this moment. Rose kept this sad truth from Eilis, knowing that if Eilis had knowledge of her illness she would never pursue her new life in America, but would want to stay in Enniscorthy. **Rose's sacrifice here is overshadowed by Eilis' sense of exclusion**, of not knowing what her sister was going through, and there is sadness in this. **Life is seen to be difficult, trying and full of sadness here.**

Rose's death makes Eilis question her move to New York. She feels she never should have left home, and this **regret darkens the mood**. This **is a sad, bleak moment for Eilis** as she suffers her grief and dislocation from home.

Telling her Mother the Truth

Eilis is very upset as she tells her mother the truth about her marriage to Tony in New York. Pushed by Miss Kelly's discovery, Eilis is prompted to tell her mother that she is returning to New York to be with her husband.

Eilis has chosen Tony over Jim, and a life in New York over one in

Enniscorthy. She has **taken control of her life** and decided what her future will be, **a decisive, forward-looking action**.

However, **Eilis' conversation with her mother detracts from her bright future**. Her secrecy about Tony suggests perhaps a lack of commitment to or belief in her marriage. Uncovering her marriage now highlights her secrecy up to this point. We may have to ask ourselves, if Eilis' future with Tony will be so happy, why has she never spoken of him to her mother until now? This reticence and **secrecy taints the outlook** here as Eilis prepares to return to her husband.

Once Eilis reveals her truth, her mother retires to bed, unwilling or unable to discuss it with Eilis. **Eilis' poor relationship with her mother and their inability to communicate meaningfully negatively impacts on the general vision and viewpoint**. Eilis is the only family her mother has in the world, yet she cannot bring herself to talk to Eilis about her husband and new life. **This is a saddening aspect of life**, that those who are so important to one another could have such imperfect relationships, and this also influences the film's outlook. **Perhaps the director is suggesting that life is not perfect, that it holds the possibility of both joy and sorrow.**

Reunited with Tony

The **film ends on a bright, hopeful note** as Eilis is reunited with Tony on a sunny New York street. Her decision has been made, her choice has been resolved, a satisfying conclusion for the viewer.

Tony is thrilled to see her, they are a young couple in love, delighted to be together again, a **positive**, warm idea.

In choosing Tony, Eilis has committed to their relationship and her life in America. There is a sense that she is really beginning her life with Tony now, having chosen him over Jim and having told her mother about him.

Eilis' words of having someone with no connection to the past, someone who is only yours, adds to the romance here. She creates the feeling that there is **something very special in this relationship,** in the fact that Tony does not belong to anyone else but her. **Eilis' commitment and emotion adds to the sense of hope and possibility for Eilis and Tony's life together.**

The final image is of Eilis and Tony together. There is the sense that **their love story will continue, an optimistic and hopeful ending.**

Theme/Issue – Relationships

Relationships has been selected as the theme/issue to explore in this text.
The theme of relationships can be applied to any relationship in a text and includes love, marriage, friendship and family bonds. When analysing this theme consider the complexities of relationships and the impact they have on characters' lives.

The relationships in *Brooklyn* and the choice Eilis must make between two men are one of the most exciting aspects of the story.

On a surface level, relationships in the film are warm and loving, with characters caring deeply about one another. Tony is smitten

with Eilis and keen to marry her, she too is much happier in New York once she becomes involved with Tony. At home too, **Eilis' relationship with Jim appears to bring her happiness**; she enjoys his company, he is sincere and loving, and his intentions of marriage show commitment.

The **problem with these relationships arises around Eilis' duplicitous behaviour.** Neither of these men knows of the other's existence, they are **unaware that they are rivals for Eilis' heart**. Eilis has secretly married Tony, **a commitment she conceals** from Jim when she returns to Enniscorthy. Similarly, she does not write to Tony, keeping her time spent with Jim a secret. **She betrays Tony by seeing Jim, and misleads Jim by keeping her marriage a secret, undermining the positive, loving aspects of these relationships.**

Secrecy and avoidance are also seen in Eilis' family relationships. Her sister Rose concealed her serious illness from her, keeping it a secret. This avoidance of the truth detracts from Eilis' otherwise warm, loving relationship with her sister. However, perhaps Rose's secrecy here is due to her wish that Eilis go and pursue a better life in New York. **She sacrifices time with her sister to ensure that Eilis makes the right choice, a selfless act.** As with other relationships in the film, **Eilis' bond with her sister is more complex than it appears at first.**

Eilis' relationship with her mother is also complex. Eilis returns from Brooklyn following Rose's death to comfort her mother, knowing it will make her mother feel better. Clearly **she loves her mother** and feels a sense of **duty and responsibility** towards her. However, **this relationship is flawed**; her mother cannot bring herself to talk about Eilis' secret marriage or life in America when Eilis reveals it to her. Eilis' interactions with her family and the problems in their relationships adds to the idea that while **relationships are superficially strong in this story, there are problems and flaws beneath the surface**, just as in

Eilis' relationships with men. Eilis is loving and happy with Tony, yet she allows Jim to pursue a relationship with her when she returns home to Enniscorthy. This raises the question of **whether Eilis really loves either man** if she can move from one to the other so quickly and easily.

It is worth considering whether Eilis would have returned to Tony if she had not been exposed by Miss Kelly. Would she have stayed in Enniscorthy with Jim if the choice was truly hers to make? Eilis' simultaneous relationships with Tony and Jim forces us to consider the strength of her love for these men. Is she a naive girl caught up in romance or does she behave selfishly in her treatment of Tony and Jim? Answering this question has a big impact on one's interpretation of the theme of relationships in this text.

Theme/Issue - Relationships
Key Moments

Rose and Eilis Talk

Eilis' close bond with her sister is seen in the scene where Eilis packs her trunk and they discuss her move to America.

Rose remarks on Eilis' meagre belongings and wishes that she could have done more for her, saying that she should have looked after her better. Clearly, **Rose feels a sense of responsibility towards her sister**. Eilis replies that what she does have is thanks to Rose. She appreciates all that her sister has done for her.

Rose says if it was just clothes and things Eilis needs, she would gladly spend every penny on her, but **she cannot buy Eilis a future. Rose truly wants what is best for Eilis**, she wants her to have every chance at success and happiness.

Eilis realises the huge distance that will be between them once she emigrates. She asks that Rose come to visit her one day. She begins to broach the topic of not seeing each other again, saying that she could not bear it, but Rose moves the conversation in another direction. **Eilis' love for and attachment to Rose is clear, just as Rose's is for Eilis. These sisters are very close and care a lot about each other**, and this aspect of their relationship is highlighted in this key moment.

Eilis Agrees to Marry Tony

Tony's proposal to Eilis is a very significant moment from the perspective of the theme of relationships. Eilis has just broken the news to Tony that she plans to return to Ireland to be with her mother following her sister's death. **While Tony is understanding of Eilis' decision, he chooses this moment to propose that they secretly wed.**

Eilis is reluctant at first, asking if a promise would not be the same thing. It appears that Tony is afraid that Eilis will not return from Ireland, and hopes to marry her to secure her return. **He tells Eilis that if she can promise then she can easily do this, a reply that is both romantic and manipulative.**

Another significant aspect of this moment is that **once Eilis agrees** to marry Tony, they go to Eilis' lodging house and **spend the night together**. It seems that in accepting Tony's marriage proposal she is also consenting to consummate their relationship.

Eilis accepting Tony's proposal shows how seriously they take their commitment to each other as deciding to marry shows that they are planning a life together.

We also see Eilis **put Tony's feelings above her own** when she does what he wants and agress to marry him despite her reluctance.

Eilis Does Not Open Tony's Letters

Once she returns to Ireland, Eilis does not speak of Tony and begins a **flirtation with Jim Farrell**, a local eligible bachelor that she meets through Nancy and George.

We see Eilis agonising over a letter from Tony before choosing to leave it unopened. She turns the letter over, before adding it to a drawer of unopened letters. Eilis' actions here are very significant as they give an insight into how she feels about her husband. **By refusing to read his correspondence, Eilis is refusing to think about him, she is forcing all thoughts of Tony out of her mind.**

Perhaps Eilis chooses not to read Tony's letters because **she feels guilty** about her developing relationship with Jim. In any case, her actions here reveal **confusion** and **a lack of commitment on Eilis' part**.

Jim Hints he will Propose

As **Jim and Eilis** dance closely together at Nancy and George's wedding they appear to be **a couple**. Jim Farrell feels very strongly towards Eilis. He has already invited her to meet his parents, and so it is unsurprising when Jim says that **he will be asking Eilis about marriage soon**.

This moment shows how Jim feels about Eilis. It also makes us think about who Eilis is committed to. When Jim suggests a future proposal, Eilis says nothing to deter him, nor does she speak of Tony, her husband. Perhaps this moment could be considered as **a betrayal of sorts** as Eilis allows Jim to falsely believe they have a future together, while simultaneously refusing to acknowledge Tony. On the other hand, perhaps she says nothing to Jim in an attempt to protect him and not hurt him. In either case, this moment adds to the **complexity of relationships** in the text.

Eilis Tells her Mother the Truth

The moment where Eilis tells her mother the truth about Tony reveals the flaws in their relationship. Eilis is upset, distraught to have kept such a significant piece of her life from her mother for so long. Eilis is telling her mother this now as Miss Kelly has revealed knowledge of Tony, her marriage is not going to stay hidden much longer, she has been **forced into telling her mother the truth**.

Eilis says that she wants to return to her husband. **She is now resolute in her commitment to Tony, despite her relationship with Jim**.

Eilis' mother is not able to talk much about Tony. She asks if he is nice, and says he must be if Eilis has married him. **Her words show her love for her daughter**. However, Eilis' mother says she is going to bed and will only say goodbye once. **This situation overwhelms her** and she cannot stay and talk with her daughter. **Sadly, Eilis' relationship with her mother is flawed by an inability to communicate openly and honestly express how they truly feel.**

Reunited with Tony

In choosing Tony, Eilis is committing to a life with him in America. Her voiceover as they are reunited speaks of **someone who is only yours** - this is **how she views Tony**, as somebody special who is hers alone, far removed from the small town gossip of Enniscorthy.

Tony and Eilis smile and warmly embrace one another. **They are happy to be together, and their reconnection demonstrates a strong commitment. Eilis has returned to Tony, he is the man she has chosen.** Any doubts she may have had no longer matter as she has returned to Brooklyn to her husband and marriage.

Hero, Heroine, Villain (Ordinary Level)

**'Hero, Heroine, Villain' refers to studying central characters (protagonists/antagonists).
Their traits, values, etc. and their ability to deal with conflict, challenges, obstacles, etc. should be considered.
Think about a character's personality, their behaviour, what you like and dislike about them, etc.**

Eilis' character undergoes a transformation over the course of the film, as she grows from an inexperienced, uncertain girl, into a determined, self-reliant woman, capable of making her own decisions and choosing her own path in life.

When we first meet Eilis, she is being controlled and spoken down to by her employer, Miss Kelly. Eilis does not stand up for herself or take her employer on. We learn that she is going to America, a decision that has been made for her, that she is happy to go along with.

The first glimpse we get of a deeper sense of Eilis' character is when she goes to a dance with her friend, Nancy and complains about the local men. **Here we see a stronger, feistier side to her that will grow over the course of the film.**

Eilis is faced with problems and heartache in New York. She misses her home and family, and finds it difficult to settle into her new life.

Applying herself to her studies, and having Tony in her life helps her to be positive about her new situation and enjoy her time in New York.

The greatest problem Eilis faces is when she becomes interested in Jim Farrell at home in Enniscorthy, having secretly married Tony in New York. Her **indecision** and **confusion** here shows her to be a very human character. She does not know which man to choose, loving both and not wanting to hurt either.

The moment for Eilis to take control of her life comes when Miss Kelly reveals that she knows Eilis is married. As her old employer tries to spitefully dominate her, **Eilis bravely stands up to her**, defiantly admitting to being a married woman. **The huge change in the way she responds to Miss Kelly shows just how much she has matured and grown since leaving the shop at the start of the film.**

Eilis returns to New York, eager and happy to start a life with Tony. She **is no longer uncertain**, fearful or homesick, but **confident and sure of the choice she has made.**

Hero, Heroine, Villain
Key Moments

Working in Miss Kelly's Shop

Our **first impression** of Eilis Lacey is when we meet her going to mass and working in Miss Kelly's shop. **She is young, quiet, courteous and obedient, and does everything asked of her**, even when Miss Kelly tells her to skip the queue to serve a well-to-do customer, Mrs Brady.

After work she breaks the news to Miss Kelly that she is going to America. Miss Kelly does not congratulate her or have anything positive to say, rather, she comments that Rose will be stuck to look after Eilis' mother. **Eilis does not speak up for herself here, but allows Miss Kelly to speak down to her.** In fact, even when Miss Kelly tells her that she need not come back to work, **Eilis is meek**, accepting this poor treatment.

Accepting Tony's Proposal

Eilis clearly cares about Tony and enjoys spending time with him, but **when he suggests marriage she seems hesitant and reluctant**. She asks Tony if a promise would not be the same thing, suggesting **she does not want to rush into this serious commitment.**

However, Tony puts pressure on her to wed, saying that if she can make a promise to him, then she can easily do this. At this point Eilis agrees to marry Tony and they spend the night together.

In this moment we see that **Eilis is not entirely true to herself. She has doubts and fears, but gives in to Tony**. This is **an example of Eilis trying to please others and putting their feelings first.** As a result she goes along with what Tony wants, rather than insisting on what she wants. This is a trait of Eilis' that crops up again and again, **she does not assert herself but gives others what they want to keep them happy.**

At the Beach with Jim, Nancy and George

When Eilis returns to Enniscorthy we see how she is maturing and growing as a person. She is more worldly and experienced than when she left home, as seen in her contemporary fashion.

When she visits the beach with Nancy, George and Jim, **her attachment to her home place is clear**. Jim tells her of a trophy the golf club will present in Rose's name. Eilis is moved by this news, her community is important to her.

She smiles and thanks Jim when he invites her to come for tea with his parents, happy to be involved in Jim's life like this. **She says that she wishes it had been like this before she went to America.** There is a sense that **she regrets ever leaving Enniscorth**y, and would be happy to stay here now. It is interesting that **she does not mention Tony**, he does not seem to be on her mind. As viewers we must consider what this tells us about Eilis - is she heartless to forget Tony like this, or is she making the best of her life in the present? In either case, **she seems happy to be home**, spending time with her friends and Jim.

She impresses the others with her "American trick" of wearing her swimming costume under her clothes, showing us that she has learned a lot in her time away.

Standing up to Miss Kelly

Eilis is polite and courteous when Miss Kelly sends for her, going to her shop to speak with her. As the conversation unfolds, Miss Kelly reveals that she knows Eilis has got married in New York. She springs this news on Eilis, trying to catch her out. **At first Eilis is evasive**, not admitting to anything, until Miss Kelly says that her new husband is Italian.

Though taken by surprise, Eilis is strong and resolute here, meeting Miss Kelly's challenge head on rather than being cowed by her old boss. Eilis says she had forgotten what the town is like, **calling out Miss Kelly's gossiping ways. She stands up for herself** and speaks back to Miss Kelly, asking her what she planned to do with this knowledge. **Eilis asserts herself here**, using her married name and calling herself Eilis Fiorello.

In this moment we see Eilis finally choosing what she wants. This is a moment of decision, of taking control in her life rather than going along with things or doing what keeps others happy. **Eilis is confident and direct in the way she deals with Miss Kelly. Her character has grown and developed** from the young, naive girl we met at the start of the film, to one that is much more mature and in control.

Telling her Mother about Tony

Eilis is upset as she breaks the news of her secret marriage to her mother. She knows that her secrecy about her marriage and her return to America will hurt her mother. Eilis grows tearful as her mother talks about her day.

The first thing Eilis says to her mother is that she is sorry, before blurting out that she has got married. She tells her mother that she should have told her when she got back, **aware of the fact that she was wrong to keep this secret from her mother**.

Here, **Eilis is open, sincere and vulnerable** as she does the difficult thing of telling her mother the truth after concealing it for so long.

She tells her mother that **she wants to be with her husband**. Having made up her mind about her future, Eilis is deeply committed to returning to Tony.

Eilis is upset and emotional in this scene. She feels regret and remorse over keeping her marriage a secret, while also appearing to miss Tony and wanting to return to him. Perhaps Eilis' tears have a number of causes, as these issues in her life come to the surface.

Her mother says goodbye to her and Eilis cries and hugs her. **Eilis cares a lot about her mother, even if their relationship is not perfect**. She cries as her mother goes up to bed, upset by all that has happened and the situation she finds herself in.

Reunited with Tony

In the film's final scene, Eilis is reunited with Tony. She has made the choice to return to New York, she is no longer carried along by what others want, but is **taking control of her life**.

In this moment, reunited with Tony on the sunny sidewalk, **Eilis is happy, content and fulfilled**. Her voiceover speaks of having someone who is unconnected to the past, someone who is only yours, and realising that this is where your life is. **This is Eilis as the film ends, committing to Tony, sure of her place and her life in New York.**

Eilis has developed as a person over the course of the film, and has grown in experience and maturity. She now knows who she is in a way she did not before. She has chosen to return to Tony and her life in America. She is doing what makes her happy in life, having become a more mature character over the course of the text.

9 781910 949825